Rich Friends, Broke Friends,

Which One Are You?
How our friends influence
our financial habits.

Kevin Caldwell

ACKNOWLEDGMENT

This book is dedicated to all of my family, friends and my mastermind group who enrich my life. Thank you for exposing me to your great ideas and uniqueness.

TABLE OF CONTENTS

Kevin Caldwell

INTRODUCTION

You know that sound, the swish of the money. The bills as they rustle against each other. Money has a feel to it; not just the special paper the U.S. Mint prints it on, or the community of people who have touched it. It feels substantial, like enterprise, and possibility. It can make or break you. So the question is—is that sound of the rustling money you hear yours, or is it your friend's? And how does your friend's money influence yours?

Maybe you've never realized this possibility. For good or bad, your friends influence you. They influence where you eat, where you shop, and how often you go out. They can even influence where you live and where you go to college. All of that involves money. But it goes deeper than that. It gets at the core of you becoming **Rich Friend** or **Broke Friend**. They each have traits are traits—learned traits that can either help or hurt you. And perhaps you are teaching some financial traits to your friends. Without even realizing it.

You'll look at your friends differently now. You will notice things you didn't notice before. When they pull out their wallet, you may wonder what's in there, or not in there. How many extra dollar bills saved, or cards with balances. Curiously, you'll discover their habits—they will come out of the woodwork and start to make sense.

After a while you'll realize, these traits would only take slight change on your part, and the result would be life changing.

PART I

RICH FRIEND TRAITS

CHAPTER 1

RICH FRIENDS PAY THEMSELVES FIRST

Rich Friends do things a little differently. Even in their 20s, they don't do things many others in their 20s thing to do. And it's not that hard.

All it took as a few minutes; just a call and visit with a financial advisor set in motion what would set Gina apart from James—she paid herself first. It was a trait that would change her life.

She seemed a little out of place in a fancy finance office. Truth be told, Gina wasn't actually rich yet. But she was following one of the traits that would make her into Rich Friend. For now, her budget was similar to others in their 20s; not money much coming in, and everything going out. But she knew investing in herself, paying herself, was non-negotiable.

So even though she didn't have much to pay herself, Gina did it anyway. And this one decision that only took a few minutes would change everything. She set up an auto withdrawal—in this case a Roth IRA—and then she just forgot about it. Even in the hard months, she worked with the budget she had leftover. Gina left her investment alone. She let it build and build.

It was slow, at first. In fact it was slow for 10 years. But giving up something once a month, just $30, a pizza and beer James had wanted her in on, a night out, that was all. Saying no now and again. It was hard at first, but then she found other fun things to do, things without money.

When she landed a better job, she would up the ante on her investment, and double it or triple it, or more, but by then she would own lots of shares. Time had been on her side all those years. And now with a better job, she could build in double time. It would eventually help make her rich.

Rich Friends, like Gina, always pay themselves first. Investing is just one way.

At the core of this trait of Gina's is an attitude of setting your limit below what you have. If you have $45 left, then just spend $40 or less. Don't believe for a second that you should spend it all; unfortunately James was accustomed to living for the day, as are so many who end up Broke. There are things Gina wants, just like everyone else, but she has patience. She knows wealth is worth waiting for.

Pile up that cash. Intentionally. Put it under your mattress, in an account that's hard to get to, or invest it automatically. Do what you have to in order to learn this trait. Eventually it'll become second nature. It will be hard at first, because you have to give up something in order to pay yourself.

For Gina, it's all about trading. Trading brands, or convenience, or impulse. Trading something temporary for something better. Instead, Gina buys what will pay her instead. An education, a long-term investment, a new business, training. Something that will pay her for the rest of her life. The margin between trades is so low. But Gina knows that choosing one over the other is what will help her win in the end. She knows it will be worth it.

So watch. See which of your friends is like Gina. Who is living below his or her means? Do you have a Gina among your friends? You'll see that her spending habits are just a little bit different. She doesn't have credit card balances. Maybe she pays with cash. Instead of buying a car using a loan and making payments, she takes the bus and then buys a car later with cash. She always waits for the right time to buy anything. She is good at waiting. She fixes appliances so they will last another few months.

See which one of your friends invests, saves every month no matter what, and doesn't spend all he has. Sometimes, he says no so that eventually he can say yes. Because se trades so he can pay himself first. And that is what makes her Rich Friend.

CHAPTER 2

RICH FRIENDS HAVE A MILLIONAIRE MENTOR

Unless you can see it, it's hard to believe that it's possible. That you can grow up to be something—something amazing. Maybe you don't come from wealth, but that doesn't mean you can't learn the traits and become that way.

Carlos and Alice are cousins. They come from families that were broke much of the time, but Carlos has a Rich Friend trait that Alice hasn't figured out yet. He has a way of seeing that wealth for him is possible. He has a Millionaire Mentor.

It seemed to happen naturally. Carlos and Alice both know this millionaire; he had been longtime friends of their families at church. This millionaire was same age as their fathers, but he knew things their dads didn't. He knew the traits to becoming rich.

Carlos could see that in the millionaire; he was intrigued by how different he was. So, Carlos would talk to him after church, about what he did for a living. After a while the millionaire offered an internship for Carlos and Alice at his company. The only catch was, they had to do the internship for no pay for three months. Carlos instantly took it; in the position he would be working side-by-side with the millionaire, learning more than money could buy. Alice was worried about money and declined, instead taking a position at a small office.

Without realizing it at first, Carlos had a Millionaire Mentor. Every day he learned about the company, how it was run, and mostly how the millionaire had built it from nothing. He, too, had been poor like Carlos. And now this millionaire wanted to pass on his knowledge to those who were willing to put forth the effort. He was charitable, but not adept to giving handouts.

"If you teach a man to fish, you feed him forever," the millionaire used to say to Carlos. Because he was with him every day, spending time with him, the millionaire's own traits rubbed off on Carlos. He realized he didn't have to stay broke. He could change his life.

So eventually, many years after the internship was over, Carlos used his knowledge gained from his Millionaire Mentor. He started his own company. When he had tough decisions, he called on his Millionaire Mentor for advice. The millionaire never gave him money, or a job, or ever offered to help him in anyway except for his knowledge. Because his knowledge, as Carlos knew, was where his wealth laid.

Knowledge, Carlos knew, was all he really needed. Who is your millionaire mentor? If you don't have one yet, get one. You'd be surprised how willing a millionaire would be to mentor you. But only if you are willing to put in the work.

CHAPTER 3

RICH FRIENDS LEARN EVERY TAX ANGLE THEY CAN

When others are scrambling to get their tax returns in, thinking about all the money they will get back and what they will do with it, Kristen is quietly thinking about the year to come. She has learned the Rich Friend trait of learning every tax angle possible.

She didn't major in tax in college, but still she took a class on it just to learn for her personal life. She reads the updates to the laws every year. And now she makes the tax code work for her, instead of the other way around.

Kristen thinks about the tax codes all year. Number one, she has the least amount taken out of her check so she can have the money each month—she adds that to her Roth IRA.

Mostly, she looks for ways to add in deductions. Since she's only in her 20s, she could just rent an apartment, but mortgage payments are deductible. So she bought a small condo and rents a room out to a friend. She has ended up paying about the same every month for a place to live, but in the long run she'll get tax deductions and profit when she eventually sells.

She has a full-time out of the house job, but Kristen knows she can add another deduction if she works at home. So she asked her boss if she could do a portion of the work at home; she's also doing some improvements to her condo, and so now she can deduct those expenses too.

Kristen and her boyfriend Warren both spend time and a little bit of cash every week doing charity work. Actually, that is where they met, and they love doing it together. One thing Warren has noticed Kristen doing is keeping track of hours and money spent. It's a Rich Friend trait she has learned in her tax classes.

You see, charity contributions, and even some time spent in charity work, are also deductible. It's not the reason why she participates, but keeping track and adding it to her tax deductions saves her from paying more taxes.

Every bit of birthday money or bonus money or money back from taxes, Kristen puts in her retirement account. It isn't the most fun way to spend it, but it's a double Rich Friend trait. Not only is she investing in herself, but the more she contributes, the more she can deduct from her taxes.

Do you only think about taxes every April, or do you consider them in decision-making all year? Which of your friends know the tax codes by heart and can help you alter some of your own habits to make the most of them?

CHAPTER 4

RICH FRIENDS WORK SMARTER

Among the rich and the broke, so many people work extremely hard. They all try their best, they stay late, and they are dedicated. But something about how Rich Friend works differs from the rest. He works *smarter*.

Aliko and Elizabeth are both sales associates at a radio station. They are similar in many ways; they are both fresh out of college, eager to build their careers in the media industry. Both are willing to learn what it takes and work hard to be successful. So far, they love working in radio.

While he works hard, Aliko has found ways to work smarter. He sells radio advertising, so a lot of what he does is approach business owners about spending money. Right away he developed a spreadsheet, and he tracks each person he contacts. This is one way he is working smarter.

Working smarter, not harder. Because he already works hard.

Aliko tracks how he approached each client, how they responded, how much they spent, etc. Basically he tracked what worked and didn't work, in hard numbers. It wasn't easy, and it was a huge eye opener, but soon he figured out the best ways to approach people and help them realize radio advertising was right for them.

It didn't take long before he was earning more money while working the same amount of hours. He also realized he was wasting time doing busywork like filing or making fliers and mailers; so he hired out for that so he could spend more time meeting with clients and making more money.

He thought bigger. He came up with fun events where he met many potential clients at once, saving him time and making him more money in less time. He was really on fire.

Elizabeth had thought she knew what worked and didn't work, just by remembering, but soon she noticed Aliko out selling her every month. Finally she asked for pointers and he told her to track everything. It wasn't long before Elizabeth took this knowledge and applied it, and it started working for her, too.

They both continued working the same hours per day, but both were smarter in how they worked. They were honest with themselves, proactive, and motivated by their successes. They hired out their busywork, and were able to focus on what made them the most money.

So keep on working hard, but look for ways to work smarter. Maybe you could streamline processes, or find new ways to do what you've always done. Instead of working late into the night, get up early, shut off social media and email and your cell, and just focus on your work.

Be productive and work smarter, not harder.

CHAPTER 5

RICH FRIENDS STAY BALANCED

Work hard, play hard. That's Carl's motto. When he isn't working in his law practice, he's climbing mountains in Bolivia, boating down the Amazon River, or jumping into pristine lakes in faraway places.

It's one of the things he does to stay balanced. Carl knows that if he gets overworked, he's no good at work. A resentful, tired, jumbled boss or employee is no good to anyone, especially himself.

A vacation is good, but Rich Friends stay balanced every day. It's the little things every day that have helped him keep a clear mind, strong body, and drive to become Rich. Here is how Carl spends most of his days:

- **He exercises every day.** Some days it's cycling, other days it's kick boxing. On the weekends he loves playing basketball with the guys. As long as he's physical every day, it's on his list. He doesn't leave it to chance; he schedules it in. What he gets in return is better sleep, better health, and a body and mind ready to work when the workday begins.

- **He keeps a detailed schedule and to-do list.** Some things must get done, and keeping track is the best way to make sure they happen. Carl does this every day, which means he reevaluates his priorities every day. He doesn't leave anything to chance—he writes it all down. Eventually he got an assistant to help him with this.

- **He gets plenty of sleep.** In order to be creative and on top of things, Carl must rest his body and mind. Going to bed early and getting up early are when his best ideas happen. So he does this as often as possible. He allows himself one late night out a week, but that's it. He schedules it usually on Friday or Saturday. But by the next night, he's back to his routine. It's how he is able to be so productive.

- **He keeps learning.** Whether it's taking a class or reading, Carl is always seeking new information, seeing what others are doing, and expanding his horizons. He subscribes to the best magazine in his industry, and he goes every quarter to a club meeting that discusses the latest information useful for his field. He is always learning and connecting with others. That is how he stays on the cutting edge.

- **He keeps things minimal.** When his house, office, and life are uncluttered, Carl can spend more time working hard and working smarter. All he brings home from his trips are pictures, and all he has to do on the weekends is laundry and a little bit of house cleaning. Then he has the rest of the time to play hard. Instead of buying more things he thinks, how much time will it take for me to care for this? Most of the time, he doesn't buy it. He has furniture, beloved art pieces on the wall, and the basics for life. It allows him more time to do what he loves.

Teresa, who works at the same office as Carl, watches as he works hard and plays hard; all her life she had thought putting in more and more hours and never taking time off was the answer to building wealth. But now she is reconsidering.

How are your Rich Friends influencing you? Are you watching them living balanced lives and wanting to be like that too? It didn't take Rich overnight to become balanced; it is something he is always working on.

Because of Rich, Teresa decided to finally start taking yoga. It's just a first step, but she's excited to make her life more balanced.

PART II

BROKE FRIEND TRAITS

CHAPTER 6

BROKE FRIENDS PAY BILLS FIRST

Li knows how to budget; at least she thinks she does. Every month she pulls out her budget notebook and writes in her expenses, and she minuses them from her income. At the end of every month, there isn't much money left after paying bills.

But she always does her duty.

After some hard experiences, Li always, always pays her bills first. She's had days without the lights on, and that one awful day when her car was repossessed, and she vowed never to let that happen again. Of course, paying your bills is good. It's responsible. It's the grown up thing to do.

But then as Li hyper-focused on paying her bills, that is all she was doing. That's why even after doing the responsible thing, she was still a Broke Friend.

Paying bills is necessary, but paying them first means you are paying yourself last. And if that happens, you will always stay broke. Because paying bills first means reacting to what is happening to you. When you pay your bills first and yourself last, you are just taking what life hands you, instead of making your life great.

Maria used to do that, until she learned from a good friend to pay herself first. She couldn't wrap her mind around the concept at first, but after practicing it for a few months, she was hooked. And after a while she was no longer broke.

That's because instead of paying bills first, she always allotted money for herself first. Cash in savings, money for investing, a little something for a big purchase later. For Broke Li, it's hard to imagine how the rest of the month will play out; but as Maria will show her, when she changes her perspective, her life changes.

It's about perspective. When you pay yourself first, your priority is not how you will get through the month—it's how you will win in the future, this month and for many months and years thereafter. This long-term outlook gives you hope. And Broke Friends can learn this from Rich Friends.

Each morning at work, Li would see how happy Maria was, and so when they became friends Li confided in Maria about being broke all the time, despite doing "everything right."

"I always pay my bills," Li told her. "What am I doing wrong?"

Maria showed her how when sitting down to budget, a simple change of paying herself first would change everything.

Of course, at first the numbers didn't work on Li's new budget. But she kept at it. Instead of going back to the old way, Li rearranged what kinds of bills she had, getting rid of a few, and eventually because of her new attitude and drive, she changed. She worked smarter, she got promoted, and her income changed.

And that's when her life changed. All the while, she kept paying herself first like Maria told her, and soon she wasn't a Broke Friend anymore.

CHAPTER 7

BROKE FRIENDS LEARN MONEY TIPS FROM MIDDLE CLASS PARENTS

The middle class is not a bad place, but it's like traffic—once you're in it, you get stuck there and it's hard to go anywhere else. That's because when you grow up that way, and you learn from middle class parents how to handle money, then it's only natural you continue in the same path.

Xavier grew up in the middle class. Decent house, yard, education, clothes. Things were happy on the surface. What he didn't know was that while they were hard working and smart, his parents were barely making their middle class existence. His parents were always stressed about money. They were Broke.

Unfortunately, so many just barely do make it, even in the middle class.

But something happened that would change Xavier forever. When the market tanked and his parents were unable to help him pay college tuition, they finally had a heart-to-heart money talk with Xavier. He was shocked to learn that they didn't have all the answers, especially about money.

He realized, thankfully not too late, that everything he had learned about money from his parents was limiting. It would keep him on a path to being middle class and Broke. That was not the place he wanted to be. He didn't want to be so consumed with money, with being Broke.

Our parents want the best for us. But sometimes, they don't have all the answers. They teach us to work hard and be responsible. Without a perspective of wealth, what they can't give us is traits for becoming Rich. Though they would if they could.

Disillusioned at this turn of events and talk with his parents, Xavier turned to his friend Carrie. She grew up rich, and from her parents she learned things she took for granted; things Xavier would never know unless he asked. Going to the same college, Carrie offered Xavier come with her on weekends when she would visit her parents. It was during these visits that he would learn from rich parents.

He would learn the traits from them that he couldn't learn from his middle class parents. There wasn't much they could do to change the path they were on, but he was only in his early 20s. He had years of opportunity ahead of him.

Eventually he was able to jump start his own life with knowledge from Carrie and her parents. It would take a lot of trial and error, and completely turning his thoughts about money around, but their influence helped him forge a new path that would change his life forever.

CHAPTER 8

BROKE FRIENDS ANTICIPATE THEIR TAX REFUNDS

Being rich for a moment—must be tax refund time.

Hillary dreams all year of what she will buy with her tax refund. She doesn't make a lot, so most everything that goes into her income taxes is given back to her most every spring. Since she doesn't save money, it's the biggest lump sums she sees all year.

Maybe she'll buy a new couch set? Or go on a cruise. What she really wants is a new wardrobe and some "play money" to buy stuff for the house, or splurging on a few nights out with friends.

Broke Friends anticipate tax refund time like it's Christmas. And since it's "found" money or "extra" money, many will use it for frivolous things. Who wants to pay down debt or save for the future with tax refund money? What fun is that?

But then Hillary had some setbacks. Her credit cards were maxed out, so she kept getting declined; her checking account was overdrawn. She had just overspent on dinner out with friends, and she still had a few days until payday and no money to buy food.

Then her car broke down and it had to let it sit in her driveway; then she realized too late that she missed paying the water bill the previous month. Enough was enough. Hillary was tired of being broke.

She had already filled out her tax return info and was waiting for it to come. This year would be different, she vowed to herself. So she invited some of her best friends over for a movie night at her house. It was fun and cheap, and something she would go on to do every month now that she was watching her budget more closely.

After the movie was over the conversation turned to money; she was surprised that so many of her friends were also anticipating their tax returns and had fun plans for how to spend the money.

Except for Alice, who stayed after everyone else had left and talked to Hillary. She said she doesn't get much money back from taxes, because she doesn't have a lot taken out of her checks; just the bare minimum deductions. That way, she gets more in her pocket every month. But instead of spending it, she had been putting it into a mutual fund account.

It's automatically deducted, so it's as if it's not even there. She set it up and just forgets about it. Until she gets her quarterly statements.

Because she's not touching it, and it's building slowly every month, she's amassed quite a nest egg. And this is separate from any retirement or savings accounts she already has. In essence, every month is "tax refund" time for Alice, in the form of slowly building, interest-earning money.

It seemed like such a radical idea to Hillary. But she wanted to be more like Alice. Frugal Alice, who bought less expensive but nice furniture on Craigslist, who didn't always go out to eat with the girls, and who at age 28 already had more in her retirement account than others owed on their student loans.

Part of that was because Alice didn't anticipate her tax refund once a year. She took the money back each month and put it to work on her own terms. That's what Rich Friends do.

CHAPTER 9

BROKE FRIENDS LET EMOTIONS RULE FINANCIAL DECISIONS

Deciding which job to take, or which college to attend, or which car or house to buy. Each is a big decision with big ramifications for your life and your financial well being now and in the years to come.

Letting emotions rule those decisions is where Broke Friends tend to find themselves.

Kelcy and Mark and their friends Zack and Jasmine make similar salaries; but one key difference is that Lisa and Mark let emotions rule their financial decisions.

They could live in the same neighborhood, since they make the same amount of money, but they don't.

Zack and Jasmine didn't necessarily want to buy an inexpensive "fixer upper" house. But they knew buying something cheap at the bottom of the market, in a few years they could make some money and upgrade. They let logic win. It isn't always easy to do, but they have run the numbers and know it will pay off in the future.

On the other hand, Kelcy and Mark instead picked a more expensive rental apartment. The finishings were nice, and they "fell in love" with the building and surroundings. The neighborhood was more upscale. They had to stretch a little to afford it, but they felt in their hearts it was worth it.

After a few years, Kelcy and Mark wondered why they were still broke and not able to afford to buy a house, while Zack and Jasmine were able to sell their newly fixed up house and buy an even nicer house in a neighborhood they wanted to be in. It had been a sacrifice, but they did it. It is because they let emotions rule their decision about where to live.

Broke Friends want what they want now, because they let their emotions rule. Rich Friends delay gratification; they are practical for a few years so later they can reach their long-term goals. How do you make big decisions? With your heart or with your head?

CHAPTER 10

BROKE FRIENDS PAY INTEREST INSTEAD OF EARNING INTEREST

The broke have a mindset of now. Flatscreen TV, iPhone, Kindle, gym membership, premium cable channels, brand name clothes, shoes he doesn't even wear, brand new appliances. Are all of these in your house?

Jack does, and he loves them All. But he's also got $8,500 in credit card debt, $24,000 in student loans, a car he owes more on than it is worth, and his rent is about $150 more than he should be spending every month. He also just had emergency gall bladder surgery; he has health insurance but it won't cover everything. He's not sure how much since the bills haven't come in yet.

He wants it all, and it wants it all right now. But he's broke. So he buys on credit. He bought his education on credit, his car on credit, and now because he can't afford those things, he's buying food on credit—just a few things here and there, like coffee and lunch out, or pizza night with the guys.

Jack doesn't think there is a problem. He'll catch up sometime. He'll get a raise, or a second job, or something will happen. He thinks he's fine, for now.

But things are pretty bad. At the rate he is going, getting deeper and deeper into debt, he'll get so behind that he'll be paying interest for years and years. It could even get so bad that he would consider bankruptcy, though it wouldn't clear his student loans.

He's pretty envious of his friend Steve. "How come you don't have any debt?" Jack asked Steve one day.

"Because I use cash."

This seemed like a foreign concept, having cash. "Where do you get it? You must earn so much more than me," Jack said.

"I save it."

After the medical bills came rolling in over the next few months, Jack knew he was in trouble. He couldn't make minimum payments on all of his debts. So he talked with Steve some more. Jack was tired of living this way. He was tired of being broke.

He learned that the reason Steve had cash was because he saved money every month, he paid cash for a practical car, he have money in his medical savings account, he budgeted for the unexpected, he invested, and he never, ever paid interest.

"Never pay interest; earn interest," he told Jack.

It took some time and a lot of sacrifice, but he learned. He cleaned up his debt, and in the meantime he didn't add to his debt. He got a second job, and he changed his habits; he changed his money traits. He moved in with his parents for a while, was able to sell his car and pay off the difference, and he paid off everything.

Now, he no longer buys on credit. He has learned to be like his friend, Steve. Instead of paying interest, he's finally earning interest. And it feels good.

CONCLUSION

Is that swish of money yours, or is it within reach? If you are a Broke Friend, do you have a Rich Friend in your midst? He or she has the traits you need to learn, so watch, ask, learn. Follow their lead. Spend less on now, and invest more in the future. Pay yourself first, and earn interest instead of paying it. Life your life in such a way that allows you to change your life for the better.

ABOUT THE AUTHOR

Kevin is one of America's leading personal achievement and performance experts. Whether keynote speaking or facilitating mastermind groups and workshops or coaching clients, audience members from America to Australia report that Kevin's high energy, refreshing and original presentations exceed their expectations. Audiences everywhere have also mentioned that their quality of life improved because Kevin coached them to break through barriers that had been holding them back from achieving their goals and realizing their truest potential.

Some of Kevin's clientele includes banks, mortgage companies, non-profit organizations, corporate executives, small business owners, media companies, judges, pro athletes, actors, attorneys, sports agents, certified coaches and many more. As a speaker, trainer or coach, Kevin focuses on organizational behavior, high performance, leadership, strategy, and entrepreneurship.

Kevin's vast array of experience includes 18 years in the Banking and Mortgage industry in various roles with government-sponsored enterprises (GSEs) like Fannie Mae, and Fortune 500 companies such as Chase, Wells Fargo, and Bank of America. Additionally Kevin has 15 years of ministry experience including several years as a Youth Pastor to over 1500 youth at The Potter's House in Dallas, TX [T.D. Jakes] where he was ranked 7th among the Nations Top 20 Youth Leaders in America. After becoming a graduate of the Devos Urban Leadership Initiative, and a founding partner of the John Maxwell Team as an independent speaker, coach and trainer, Kevin started Project Me Coaching, a self- development practice and a high performance consultancy for organizations, individuals, and teams that want to increase employee performance, motivation, engagement, and retention. Additionally, Project Me assists individuals and organizations on their journey to reaching their truest potential, revealing the best version of themselves.

Kevin's philosophy is that success is not measured by the positions you have reached in life, but what mental obstacles you overcame to reach your desired goal. Using this philosophy, Kevin has written several books that are available on amazon.com. Check all of them out on the next page.

Kevin is committed helping individuals and organizations increase their personal velocity—which he defines as their ability to get where they want to go faster, safer, and happier. Through his passion for excellence and innovative approach to life he has garnered many rewarding experiences, but Kevin's most passionate pursuit is to be the best father he can be to his amazing gift from God, his daughter, Imani.

For more info about Kevin visit www.thekevincaldwell.com or @kevincaldwell on twitter